COCKTAIL BIT

Kate Collier is a Sussex-based pub poet who is passionate about building local community through the spoken word and inspiring others to share their thoughts, feelings and sense of this challenging, changing world in their own way. The youngest of seven, she knows how hard it is to feel your voice matters too.

When times feel dark, Kate sees the natural world as the restorer of the imbalance we have created, ever-forgiving of who we humans are, and forever willing to sustain us. No better time than now for us to truly listen - and give back.

These are her first published poems. She read the poem she wrote on the second day of lockdown on Radio 3's 'The Verb'. She runs and performs as Allie Rocket – an anagram of her name – at a monthly poetry and music pub evening in Shoreham-by-Sea, where she lives.

Cocktail Bitter & Sweet

Kate Collier
(aka Allie Rocket -Pub Poet)

THE REAL PRESS
www.therealpress.co.uk

Published in 2021 by the Real Press.
www.therealpress.co.uk
© KateCollier

The moral right of Kate Collier to be identified as the author of this work has been asserted in accordance with the Copyright, Designs and Patents Acts of 1988.

All rights reserved. No part of this publication may be reproduced, stored in a retrieval system or transmitted in any form or by any means, electronic, mechanical or photocopying, recording, or otherwise for commercial purposes without the prior permission of the publisher. No responsibility can be accepted by the publisher for action taken as a result of information contained in this publication.

ISBN (print) 9781912119097
ISBN (ebooks) 97s81912119080

Illustrations by Jackie Gordon (Instagram: jackie_gordon1963)

Thank you to my dear sons, Tom and Chris Heaphy, who have watched me grow as I have them. Also to their loving father Terry who has sadly missed our last twenty years (or maybe not).

Contents

Section 1 The First Wave

Anthracite Night -   11
A Dream Before the Virus Came - 14
Two Days before Lockdown -   17
Mother Nature - Lockdown Day 1   - 18
Allie Rocket - 20
We can't meet at all - 24
The Zoom Rush - 25
All rolled into one -Lockdown Day 2 - 27
Only Day 4 - 29
A Tale of Two Cities - 31
My Birthday – Lockdown Day 5 - 32
Exercise & Shop Walk – Day 7 - 34
Trembling with love…. -   36
A Minute's Silence for health workers - 37
Lucky Charms - 40
The Language of War - 42
Pillow Bound -   44
On a Bad Day -   45
Mr DC   -   47
Parallel Worlds -   50

WD40 - 52
The Candelabra - 54
More Needs to be Less - 55
Easter Weekend - 59
Shifting wakeful weed - 61
Unpick Time - 62
A Sonnet to Lockdown Love - 64
Platitudes hold Attitudes - 65
I can't breathe – Day 74 - 67
Black is the Colour - 69
Bubble Support - 71

Section 2 Between Waves

Corkscrew Curled - 75
Doing Denial - 77
A Midsummer Prayer - 78
A Three Sticks of Make-up Rule - 80
Miners of Gold - 81
Barefooted - 83
A kind of Identity Rap - 84
Laugharne, Wales Aug 2020 - 87
Laugharne 2 - 90
Berlin Ten Days Ago - 93
Unlocking Waterstones - 95

The Old Apple Tree - 97

Section 3 Tiers of Tears

Just Bellow   -   102
Humour Me   -   104
Perished at Sea - 106
A Sleep Memory – Khartoum 1978 - 110
Lockdown Recipe   -   112
The Dance of Intimacy   -   114
Forbidden Fruit -   116
Anger   -   118

Section 4 – No Endgame

Shifting –ion -   121
Cocktail Bitter and Sweet -   122
Porridge Jan 2021   -   123
The Portal -   124
Silent soft space -   125
Stained Glass Man   -   127
Cot Poems - 129
Water - 131
Kimonos, Bears and Milonga   -   135

Unmasked - 137
The Magic of a Can of Spray - 139
Salvage - 142
Winter Swim - 143
The Moon is mourning - 145
Cod Liver Oil and Frogspawn - 146

Other poems

Lockdown Fantasy - 151
Guitar Pick - 153
Roses are Red, my Love - 154
My Pesce Way - 156
Gallahers - 159
A Shepherd Woman in Wales - 161
Stones - 163
FOMO and JOMO - 166
Masks, Hips and X-Rays - 168
23 Inches Wide - 169
A Song to the Willow - 171

Introduction

This all started in a local pub in my home town, Shoreham- by- Sea, three years ago. I was asked to read my poems) every month. It was in the asking that the poems started rolling out sometimes in those waking hours, or just in the rhythm and rhyme of my step as I walked in the street stopping to get them down fast.

I was the youngest of seven children and I guess I took a long time to get going, but I always loved reading poetry as my father did. The 'smallest room' was the one place where I could have the silence and space to do so, much to the annoyance of those waiting to get in there!

Now in my late sixties, I find myself on a poetry platform with a lifetime of things to say that will no longer wait. One day in that pub, someone just called me a poet. I reckon that's it then! Without any pretensions, I'll be just that – a pub poet and, whatever such a label means, more than anything, just be who I am.

This selection reflects the many poems that came daily during a worldwide pandemic and the inevitable lockdown. These are partly my own voice and partly the voices of others around me. They are interspersed with poems unrelated to these times. Many people live by the sea for their close affinity with water. I am one of them and the sea is the subject of many of the poems.

The two penultimate poems reflect attitudes to disability, a subject dear to my heart. I welcome a world where we are all respected for what we bring to life, where we all see ourselves in some way as differently-abled and are given the opportunity to live equally. Isn't that the richness of diversity?

I thank my editor Simon Zec at the Real Press for starting this whole thing off, all my fellow poets and musicians in AP & Pickering's collective. We said goodbye to our live pub evenings in early 2020 and met in our Zoom Pub over the last eighteen months bringing a lot of creative fun to lockdown. I met two excellent Wolverhampton performance poets, Emma Purshouse and Steve Pottinger, in a pub in Brighton two years ago and thank them for encouraging me with their online course and events.

I was fortunate to find in my illustrator, Jackie Gordon, a very intuitive artist who resonated with my poems and enjoyed working creatively with this small collection. Thank you, Jackie.

I also want to thank my close friends and those in my family who encouraged me. You know who you are.

Bring your own voice to the poems you enjoy and make them your own. Forget those you don't.

Kate Collier
(Pub Poet - Allie Rocket)

Section 1:

THE FIRST WAVE

Anthracite Night
Camping on the Serengeti, Jan 2020

He said to us as cool as can be
If you're up in the night
have your head torch on
not on red but white
make sure it's shining batteries working
and if you meet a lion

look him in the eye no trace of fear
just fix him squarely
then step back slowly
and shine your torch till his eyes turn to stone.
A bright light is alien to a lion's sight
Trust he'll turn around and leave you alone.

It's a heart thing to hear a lion roar
Exhilarating yet scares you to the very core
waking you in the anthracite night
It vibrates through your body
high on alert
as you sleep on this African earth.

You lie in your tent petrified
Don't open your vent and woe betide
if you unzip and look outside
and all you want to do is hide
in your canvas home with a fragile wall
There's a lion on the other side

you can feel your tent moving
feel your tent moving, don't call
keep silent. He owns it all
this vast open plain of the Serengeti
is his after all.
The lion he still remains king
and you are only visiting.

It's a heart thing to hear a lion roar
It scares you to the very core
But you're in a tent that looks like a rock
and he's passing through
just taking stock, marking what's his
before the sun comes up

I'll always hear that lion's roar
It's stored in here forever more
There's a rumble of an elephant
stamping on the ground

But the earth it still trembles as I hear the sound of the king of the jungle on his round.

A dream before the virus came

Thick rubber bands
circles on the street
brown thrown down
the postman tears the letters from the stack
delivers to odd-numbered doors
read or unread.
Bands joined up tail to head
pavement flown
they shiver and squirm in rubberised form
and our feet skip a beat
as we see a worm.

Even the birds in this muse are confused.

In a strange kind of way
rubber bands feel safe:
they hold things together
stop them floating away.
And the floods will come one day
with rivers in the streets
comforts all gone
cold hands in the water and

in the debris we'll discover
the postman's rubber band
familiar and strong.
It'll hold us together
in a circle of rubber
a buoyancy float for the young
Like bands of friendship helping us weather
a future imagined now gone.

And we need to be fish again
In that way we could still belong.

Two days before Lockdown

Can you spare me two sheets of toilet roll, sir?
I waited awhile and I didn't stockpile
but I went down the aisle of the shop today
And all I could see looking at me were
metal shelves with nothing there
stripped bare of products of any kind
everything taken selfishly
in our me, me, me society
that I stupidly thought we'd left behind.
No bleach, no soap, just rows of despair
for those who care that
everyone has their share;
others who can't cope
with the frenzy and fear
hold back and wait till there's nothing there
and like old Mother Hubbard
find their cupboard is bare.
Can you spare me two sheets of toilet roll sir
I hold out my wooden begging bowl
It seems there's nothing there.

Mother Nature
Lockdown Day 1

"Oh please Mother Nature, tell us for sure:
Is this Covid-19 the way you'll cure all that we've done
Try to restore what we now see and we can't renew
Guess we've gone too far with our needs and our greed
so you're planting the seed of something different
Finding redress for human excess
Giving this sky you hold so dear
a rest from the planes that pollute the air.

Hardly fair for the trees we breathe
So you ground us all take away our control
empty the trains, the buses, the cars
stop the fuel that pollutes and destroys
soils our water, tars the lungs
of the earth we need to respect to belong.

Do you think we own it like a possession
make a division between humans and nature
a kind of derision? It is our delusion.

No movement of rebellion at impending extinction
can do it fast enough.
We're running out of time. Hear the ticking of the
   clock?
We just can't take stock in the time we've got
to break this culture that wants so much."

So who comes along but Mother Nature,
in her woven cloak golden and
glistening threadbare but still here.
It's a time to listen, to listen deep
however hard her words, however harsh she speaks.

"You've plundered and squandered what's mine by
   right
Gone on your flights just when you liked
Driven without thought, carbon spurting out
Not thinking what it's been like for
me to see the sky filled with filth
where once it was clean and my mountains seen.
You've spilled oil in my seas, taken life killed in
   plastic
And there in the tropics cut down forests for
   consumption
With no thought or mention for what I hold dear,
that grows and lives there.

So I sent you the warnings and asked you to change
earthquakes, tornados, floods, storms and deluge
but you kept on destroying with your godlike brains
all your science, inventions, and high speed
    consumption
your economic structure based on power and greed.
You just couldn't stop, you knew it was insane.
And now you ask for refuge
from this virus that you fear
which will clean my air and bring human tears
clear the addiction to selfish want, make you fall so
flat you have to be in a place
where you listen to me

and see
that your body, your psyche,
the earth you live on
that revolves each day round the warmth of the sun
- it is all one.
The animals, the birds lost and gone
the mountains, the seas, the trees that are our lungs
every living thing isn't treated differently
it all has a claim, equal and the same.

So, I'll bring this virus under duress
to tame human greed and selfish excess

I'll protect this planet from much, much worse
And stop this polluting mess."

Allie Rocket

I was rattling my brain for an interesting name
Something to feel anonymous
Well nothing came.
So I skyped my son Tom and in a split second
he took my name and scrabbled it up.
He said Allie Rocket. I told him I loved it
then he reckoned I couldn't call myself that.

My son made it up then said You can't, Mum!
It isn't serious, isn't really very cool
I said I don't care I won't follow all that
I'm just a pub poet after all and
you know I don't do cool.

Tom laughed said What did I think
if we changed Allie Rocket to Ollie Racket?
I said Stop it. I've had enough.
If you muddle me up I'm bound to forget
say Ollie not Allie and Racket not Rocket
So fuck it I'll take it and make it my name.

Well, I didn't say that, but something more tame.

We can't meet at all
March 2020

Oh hell! I'm here by the rails again
There's a blast of a wind and it's pouring with rain
I can't see a train in sight down the line
I'm swearing to myself under my breath
at the signals, and getting wet. It's all in vain.
So I might as well just wait stay still
keep mindful - a bit - and read the posters
tied to the railings: Welly Live Music coming up
cutting air pollution from Extinction Rebellion
a Craft-making class, another Stained Glass
Event at the Ropetackle Film on next week.

They're all redundant not done but gone
washed away in the rain in a lockdown rule
and the tears of what's happening to us all.

Except perhaps cutting your engine, your fuel
but the cars have gone quiet, none about
and the few that are exercising, walking to get out
are gathering now.

We wait at the gate for the train to go by
silenced by the shock of it all
and trying to learn the distance rule.

I phone a friend to say I'll be late
then break the call clean forgotten
we can't meet at all.
Just in one day our lives have changed
and now we can't meet at all.

The Zoom Rush

On an ordinary day
in an ordinary time
there are ordinary jobs
normal hours 9-5
regular weather
forecast wind and light showers.
You moan a bit, groan a bit
coffee breaks together
swap gossip and the odd bit of banter.
Now this virus has hit
and everything's changed
suddenly.
We've all joined Zoom
and found ourselves rooms
for greetings with mates and online dates
business meetings and family times.
Cyber ways to communicate
keep us together through isolating days
creating activities online. Important
but really not quite the same - all this
muting, unmuting, sharing a screen
sitting in a gallery frame

with our name for an identity.
We're isolated in private rooms
now seen by all publicly
yet fused together from the waist up
dependent on servers
and service providers
in pathways jammed with internet users
a new ordinary.
Oh, for this technology
and all the dichotomy
enslaving us and yet setting us free
in a new mixed ecology.

Is this how the world is going to be
our new normality, new ordinary?
Guess we can only wait and see.

All rolled into one
Lockdown Day 2
**as read on Radio 3 The Verb,
 on 17 April 2020**

I could write a thousand poems all rolled into one
and see where it goes, see where it runs.
It could start with the sky where there's no sound of planes
how the air feels fresher
and it's got a new colour
with no sign of stains
making streaks of white
that cross overhead from morning to night.
Those stains of flight
fine strands of floss
that weave and crisscross
like trails blazed in times of old
on Navajo paths searching for gold.
Lift your eyes arching and scan the sky
you won't see them now
not one line of travel
no patterns to trace, no string to unravel
just all blue with sunshine

a healthy sign
and the birds that fly high
preened and clean.
I could write a thousand poems all rolled into one
and see where it goes, see where it runs
but today I'll just stay with the sky and the sun.

Only Day 4

Is it Day 4 of captivity
when you reach the layer you don't want to see
where however much sunlight there is outside
there's a shadow at your side
making you sombre where the light has no answer?
Where all of the tools you've gathered together
to keep you well, avoid going under
no longer work, tell you it's a cover
to avoid the fractures deep within
buried and carried for such a long time
where the others around you
just trigger it all
and you lie prostrate on the floor
knowing right now you can't go on
can't do any more?

You just lie in the shadow
you have no strength
for the cheery platitudes
your friends have sent
to make you feel better
keep strong through this lockdown

they just make you compare
just add to the feeling
Day 4 is your meltdown.

And while some talk of sorting their sheds
you feel just worse can't do it somehow
can't hold it together, don't want to join in
the collective smile fixed with superglue
which we use to get through.
The glue doesn't stick
only works for a while
then you come to that day
when the smile meets its shadow
and you can't deny you feel hollow inside
today just empty
emptied out.

A Tale of Two Cities

It's sad not to see you anymore.
For the time to still stop suddenly.
That words change their order
the silence gets louder
and you are no longer my safety.
The door's up locked
no longer ajar
and our star at night
looks down from afar
as we both sit in rooms separately
in a tale of two cities
many miles apart physically
no metres apart in our heart.
No nothing words or trivial talk
No hug to share
No hand in hand walk
on those weekends together
are they gone for ever?
Just a screen breaking up
as we disconnect. Is that it?
Will lockdown go on so long
we soon forget how we met?

My Birthday: March 27
Lockdown Day 5

Does it actually really matter
Do I really have to bother?
I'm not going anywhere, so who cares
it's my birthday – but with all of this,
who cares how I look?
Some exercise maybe around the block
But no-one will see me anyway
They say keep the lockdown, don't they?

Then I stop for a moment and think
hold on, don't talk like that
Don't you dare be someone you're not
you forgot this woman
who loves colours bright and bold
the blues, the greens, the pinks and the gold.

Are you going to suddenly
make her grey and give up on her
special day, self-isolated and on home-stay?
The birds are singing chirping away
building their nests with light returning

new life with spring, hope in the making
and nothing, no nothing can take that away.

How about this one as good as new?
Bit chilly today I'll wear that one too
If I put something pink on and then something blue
I'll cheer myself up
for that online view.
Perhaps a bit of red lipstick too.

And in that moment
I feel a kind of pleasure
time off from the fear
I try to deny lurks somewhere in there.

One thing normal, slowed down
in the moments between moments
this choosing what you wear
seems the one thing planned
an ounce of control where
there's none elsewhere.

Exercise & Shop Walk
Lockdown Day 7

The sea sparkles, glimmers today
like shimmering liquid silver,
dappled with grey
The sea she's wearing her jewellery
a kind of watery majesty
and we're out getting our Vitamin D.

And the blades in the wind on the horizon
that bring us all electricity
still turn in motion
giants of steel
waving their arms
like an out of season Catherine wheel
They talk to each other
two metres apart it seems to me
though I guess it's more like thirty –
the sun is bright and it's hard to judge
from where I sit on the pebbled beach
looking out to sea.

And I stay still as the waves so gentle
more like a ripple
curl themselves over
turn themselves inwards
in the sun's silver
bring themselves closer
wet sand and water
whispering to us
muffled by the bitter cold wind
that bites our skin
midday in spring
when the clock has turned
and the light bleaches the darkness out.

And the only sound on top of this
are of pebbles thrown
stone upon stone
where my son, Chris,
sits next to me, looking
for dolphins out at sea.

...trembling with love...

Sometimes I wake trembling with love,
and in the rambling moments of
my sleepy mind,
where the unconscious flirts with the conscious
and the mental seduction,
finds thoughts not yet shaped
to the daily plan gone anyway
in this new land.

In those moments,
early - very early -
I know he's there
with me,
lays beside me,
reassuringly
trembling with love.

That's on a good day.

A Minute's Silence – for health workers who have died

Poem 1

At 11 am this morning
in the silence,
with our hearts boiling
at so many dying
please don't let our anger
cover the grieving
that those in their caring
in their departing
deserve from us right now.

Poem 2

To those who stay young
who will not have my time
I promise to bring in my small way
what we who have suffered differently
see is needed right now.

There's a time to be angry
a time to be sad
a time to be good
a time to be bad
a time to worry
a time to be sorry
all human together
our wild needs unmet
crawling on knees across this earth
our secrets of yearning unknown yet.
And for those who died young
in our life's fading
with autumn leaves falling
we can step out the hero
find the fears and the tears
where the suffering we feel
is food for our need
to grow in knowing
bold and true.
We can strike a path
for those who stayed young
leave our masks behind
those we've always put on
and with feet on the ground
our hearts can soar high
where we find as we fly

in the sound of the wind
something different and new.
Something for those who will never know.

Lucky Charms

Flash of goldfinches
in the garden
flying good luck charms
a bird's lockdown wish
to protect us from harm.

Gold glint mixed with red
and black in the feather
bold windy weather
rapid flutter of wings brings
a brushed-up touch.

A rush from cherry
tree to pond flitting
to dip in the water baths
shaped in an eight
they steady the flow
heaven's tears don't know.

As they line up with sparrows
in pick-pecking order
splash one another everywhere

then duck and cover
and dash elsewhere.

The Language of War

Can we diffuse the language of war
Of course we're "fighting" Covid-19
but we seem to be taking it far too far
and then we're in fear of not saying
what we think, sounding mean
even seen to be unpatriotic
when it's a *worldwide* pandemic.

There's something not right in this talk about fight.
NHS workers sent into battle, no arms to defend,
no PPE
Called frontline workers like frontline soldiers
who traumatised at the end of the battle
will probably be given CBT
A medical model quick fix solution
sticking salve and plaster over trauma
only resolved somatically.

These "heroes" are victims of underfunding
from a government who had the warning
and did nothing. Frankly, it's shocking.
So I ask you to tell me this?

How many expressions in this poem
could fuel the worst kind of nationalism?
Can we reframe, be aware
not inflame a serious condition
with words that take us in the wrong direction
from the change we need. Daring the compassion
to share our global fragility.

Pillow Bound
Lockdown Day 38

'Slide to power off' as my finger runs across and I
close the screen like you draw the curtains
habitual round as the day ends
and darkness descends,
sends my phone into slumber
where no text or number can be found
where the 'infodemic' is another pandemic
and the horror of BBC news put down
slips from my hand
by my bed on the floor
so I can give rest to over-wording
hear no beeps any more
close the door on it all
sleep in silent sound calling
a round of yawning dream-states dawning
I'm folded in duvet pillow-bound
Tomorrow I'll cope with my next lockdown day.

On a Bad Day

I put on a mask in an empty shop -
Blind without glasses,
Deaf without aids
Blind and deaf, but not yet dumb.
So I pick up this mask
and my very first task
is to work out how I put it on.
Is it back of the head or over the ears
white or blue at the front?
And I fight back the tears of this Covid thing
that's hitting me suddenly physically -
I mean what's left of me?

My glasses steam up as I go in the shop.
I really can't see and that's getting at me.
And then there's the vanity -
This mask is no beauty, certainly
All the stylish ones are already out of stock
And it looks like my face is wearing a sock.

I'm returning a parcel that needs a label
Printed in the shop with a QR scan

I'm already fed up I can't print it at home
Not a fan of all these apps on my phone.
Well I scan this code and it won't match up
and my mask's gone skew-whiff
is starting to lift over my eyes, rise up.
The man from the till comes over to me
he helps me position this crazy QR
"...bring it down and towards you
stand a bit away...no...stop not too far
now nearer your middle just a bit lower..."
And I fiddle to get the precision exact
with a mask on my face that feels like a sack.

What a prize fool at something so small
I get behind the line now
and queue where there isn't a queue
trying to breathe through it all.
I'm for sure a claustrophobic
in a bit of a panic
and the only thing making me
human right now
is the thanks that I give
in my voice and my smile
which I'm sure he can't hear
and I know he can't see
and the smiles I give are important to me.

The final straw
is walking out of that store
As I whip my mask off
it gets tangled up
and one of my hearing aids pops off
So I pick it up off the street in a right old huff
moaning and swearing at all this stuff
we have to do now just to live somehow.

Knowing I could be in much worse a place
does not take away my mood today
My smile has gone without a trace
and with my mask off it shows on my face.

Mr DC

Life unwrapped in our two metre rule
And life is a distance between us all
Shifting places walking paces
something comic about our faces
robots in human bodies ordered
it just has to be...
And it's taking over our psyche
so we see 2 meters everywhere
in the distance between two trees
In the wind turbines far out at sea
In the cat's eyes on the motorway
when we're driving full belt to our family
I'm talking about a Mr DC.
Perhaps now I wonder
when leaders some manic
who have their own rules
in a gut of panic
want to control to get a grip on it all
and tell us to stay at home on alert
while they drive to places they shouldn't go
steal all we've lost in pain and grief
the recovery in the next few weeks.
Can we trust what they ask us to do any more

when some are prepared to flout the law?
And can you write a poem in the rule of rhyme
When someone acts against what's asked at this time.
I feel disrespected and undermined.

Parallel Worlds

Sitting by the pond tea in my hand
there's something submerged
Curled in the water
wind gently blows
it pops up all sinister
then down and under,
head like a monster
alive with the breeze
and I check again.
It isn't a frog and it isn't a newt
and in this small pond
this micro world of reeds and weeds
I suddenly see that monster of fame
we all can name easily.
The one from Loch Ness
feeding on fish or larger stock
Not fish at all just imagery
and tadpoles that wriggle
on the smooth shiny dish
of an unopened lily pad
there I see that ancient loch story

Is it myth or mystery?
A head in a photo so blurred we can't see
Local legend for the tourist to come
buy souvenirs and down the whisky
And as I squint in the sun to see
I have this visual fantasy
There's a parallel world in this dugout pond
And in the mud on the bottom there lies
a shrivelled old reed long since died
emerging from under spring life
Curled and unfurled with a reptile shaped head
trapped in prehistory
Nothing unusual actually
no myth no mystery.

So I go back to my hot cup of tea.

WD40

Is it a lock-in
Or are we locked up,
a lock down, down locked,
Or found housebound as such
Much like a homestay?
Maybe on your own
so you're home alone
Or if you're together
confinada en casa -
Well actually whatever
you're a stay-at-home
with a no exit sign
until the time when they find the key
and how many keys will they have to cut
to unlock the whole of this country?
And how many locksmiths will it take
to break open the locks that have seized up?
So toilet tissue is no longer an issue
but be aware as we prepare
a locked down break free plan
If we don't want to risk a longer stay

better stock up and grease that lock
with the blue and yellow convenience can -
that magical WD40.

The Candelabra

We walk in the park
at the end of the day -
sky still blue with a white patch or two
and surrounding us
the trees in the spring
bow their heads and sing
to the chestnut tree
majestic and tall
the great Candelabra of them all.
Adorned with cream candles on every branch
the large green leaves shiver
with the light shining through
the trees shimmer, we walk down under
in the sun's setting
see the dappled glimmer
as the light gets dimmer.
As if from a cue
with the day nearly over
while she prepares to bed herself down
the rays of the sun nearly gone
light each candle one by one.
A message of healing

a tree's time for hoping
that this earth can restore
not return to before
but something more.
And the flowers unfurled
candles lit by the sun
mark a way for the world
as dark blankets all
and the day is over and done.

More needs to be less
Lockdown Day 38

This house still needs sorting.
It's such a mess -
More needs to be less.
I've meant to do it for so long now
just keep somehow delaying it all
More interesting things occupy me,
but

still it's here, still I see
Files to clear, books to pass on
Out of date letters over and gone
And I've got no space
For all this stuff
I want to keep simple,
but

more needs to be less.
it's causing me stress -
The office, the attic
The things I keep
The things I hold from a past that's old

need to be thrown, free-cycled or sold,
but

I'm exhausted today
with all my intentions
perhaps in Week 7, I'll start to declutter -
and maybe under this junk reverie,
I'll find me.

Easter Weekend

Easter weekend here again -
old things gone, new beginnings
darkness leaving our winter bones
the death rattle of this cold season -
bringing hope.

Marking of seasons inside and out
clear the clutter, chuck it out;
the shedding of skin
sombre clothes change to brighter -
lifting the mood.

It goes without saying it's different:
this year, we dwell on death,
feel some fear that somehow
we may have gone far too far,
despair some will be treated differently

where there lies captive poverty
with years of invasive inequality.
Or where people camp as refugees
knowing two metres apart

is a privileged place
far from the cramp of such camps.

But you know
we have to stand tall, save the day
falling to victim doesn't help
it's just a way to cover the hurt
stops us from finding another way.

So it might sound too easy
but if any of us are left in this country
while they're still talking herd immunity,
I just need to say

That, in the freedom of something different,
we hold a dream, a dream that's new.
Great movements of change have
happened that way and without
a dream fresh and scary,
nothing in this world comes true.

Shifting wakeful weed

She swims early, eyes half open,
shifting weed from stormy seas,
sifting seeds of southwest winds
silent suffering joy slow waking,
the cold sting in her half-woken strokes
bringing a life and tingling.
Wrapping her skin in a warm towel, now
dreaming from her lockdown room
she's fully awake as her day begins.
The sea will call her soon.

Unpick Time

I'm unknotting myself
to knit myself new -
Unpicking rows with too much tension
others that are too loose.
What else can I do
in this lockdown time
but search the lines for a new
pace and time
meaning, rhythm, rhyme?
To find a style of pearl and plain
a regular pattern to keep myself sane
with the hope we can knit together again
hear the needles click in an untick time
warming the heart
in a new way, awake to each day.
What else can we do but
discover a pattern we can knit together
uncover our hearts to something new
me and you,
to get us through.

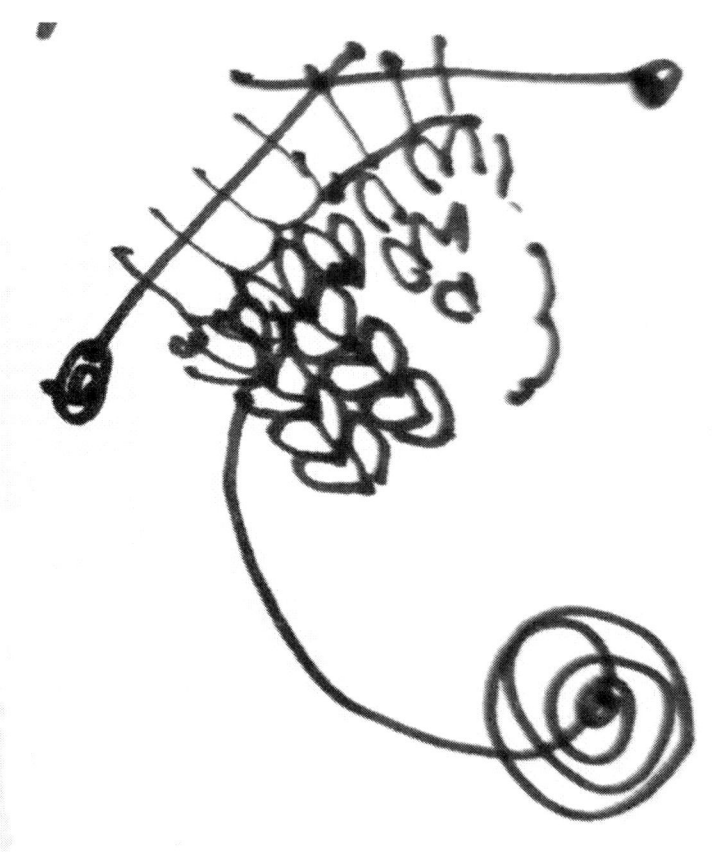

A Sonnet to Lockdown Love

Shall I compare thee to a Lockdown Day?
Thou art more handsome and considerate -
Indeed, thou art more bold and intimate,
You vow you will not take my rights away
Or keep me in a darkened room all day.
But I for one must surely resolute stay,
not hold false dreams that we may go away.
Not close together in a far flung land,
Nor walking in the sunset hand in hand -
Though I be tempted by a hug and kiss,
I know that it would be of me remiss,
I hold my honour, duty to resist,
When actually what I want to do much more
Is spend some time with you and just get pissed.

Platitudes hold Attitudes

Lashings of positivity
Lush as such
But not much for the people on lockdown today
not feeling good
pushed into positivity
by what 'you' think and then say 'we'
it has a bit of a feel-good bully.

And I see it on Facebook constantly
Someone who thinks it's their role in life
to cheer us up
in this time we're in
someone who shows how wise they are with quotes
and sayings
playing on those who don't want to know
posting others voices from well-known sources
not letting them own the mood they're in.

They may be helpful when we're on top
but not when we're down with our head in the bin.

When I say all this I feel good right now
Lush as such
And nothing wrong with some positive vibes
but insisting on them and judging what is
well it's time for some sensitivity
platitudes hold attitudes
you're trying to get another to see
when actually they feel lousy.

Does it make you feel better
to rescue another, stop your pain
post positive sayings again and again
when any attempt will appear cliché
a Facebook washing of brain
to rescue another with food and spin
make them feel shame?
When just for today
a black cloud is covering
whatever you say
and the sun simply won't get in.

I can't breathe
Lockdown Day 74

I can't breathe. I can't breathe.
You're hearing it repeated again and again
I'm white and I'm hearing it too.
Take your knee off our neck -
That's all you're asking.
I'm white and asking that too
You won't suffer in silence you're loudly saying
I'm white and saying it loudly too
You're rejecting this unequal legal system
I'm white and rejecting it too.
You're nodding as one shouts no justice no peace
I'm white and I'm nodding too.
You recommit to the King's pledge and dream
I'm white and I recommit too.
You ask for no judging of colour of skin
I'm white and I'm asking that too.
You're pleading for an end to injustice
I'm white and I'm pleading too.
You're raising you're hand to say never again
I'm white and I'm raising mine too.
You're taking the knee to stop racism

Kneeling at 8 pm on the street pavement
We're white and we're kneeling too.
You're calling for a better world
I'm white and I call for that too.
And here I stand white
And I have no right
to stand behind and beside you
as you rise up
And yet I do.
I mean, the whole point is
we're all, we are all
Human after all.

Black is the colour

On these warm nights in May,
as the sun goes down,
and the bright cloudless day
fades to deep dark blue,
a crescent moon plays with stars in the sky
and a single blackbird perched high on a mast
sings a solitary aria -
pure and clear in perfect note,
melancholy to me.

It tells of the past that never lasts,
that's already gone in the pause of the song.
It brings hope in refrain a peace again
And, where there's anger, a sadness and pain
at the trauma inflicted
by men who are wounded in infancy
find hearts of stone and loins of iron so early.

The wounds of injustice the hatred and stain
the unhealthy minds of men who are blind,
who can hold a man perversely restrain
till the life has gone and what remains

is anger and fury battle and blood
to fight the old story.
Inequality surfaced again.

Black and White together now -
young arms linked in chains,
Saying NO, NO, NO never again,
And the streets of America still
ripped apart with these men of authority,
full of superiority, frozen by bigotry.

As we feel the heat in the bloodied streets,
this blackbird sings of black being black
and the beauty in his tenor tones
brings a ray of light in -
in the crack of what we lack.

Bubble Support
Lockdown Day 80

You want to form a bubble with me?
And is that bubble a he and a she
Or a he and a he or a she and a she,
which makes it a bubble of we
If he forms a bubble with me:
then he can't form a bubble with you.
Double bubbles will only cause trouble -
so whatever the wobble
just stick to one bubble.
No we're not talking bubbles
out of a bottle
Not bubbles you blow
but where you can go
to be with another -
A place to take cover
crack that cabin fever
of lockdown tether
to babble away and be
with friends or lovers or family.
So well, shall we do it
as the government say

with their latest thought of the day
Let's make a bubble the unlock way.

Section 2:

BETWEEN WAVES

Corkscrew Curled

A shell lies on the shore
And this is the one I see
Among so many

Close to the water's edge
White with a tinge of pink on the rim
Long thin and corkscrew curled
Digging into the white bleached sand.

A wave sweeps it up drags it further out
I lose it for that silent second or two
Between one wave and another
Then catch it again
This delicate shell lands high
on the line of foam
between wet and dry
Intact

Wrapped in a strand of seaweed
wrinkled shine of iron brown
with pocket eyes like bubble wrap you want
to pick up and pop as a child.

Is there a creature in there?
I gently turn it and see
shaping the spiral in my fingers.
It's empty
an empty shell
The one who lived in there
has left.

Doing Denial

Dark clouds descending
descending on her
in the pain and agony
she feels her bones -
there's no pretending
she's sitting alone.

No getting up and making good
No carrying on with a stoical smile
No cheering up others just to deny
the grief of this virus carried inside.

I don't know about others
but it doesn't fool me.
I hear in the chat
that I have with my friends
an honesty
that this grief won't hide so easily.

It carries a weird kind of recipe
The mix of relief and the sense of fear
unlocking

just hangs in the air.

There's joy and frenzy back on the run
with hundreds hitting beaches,
weeks held inside -
they need to come, need to have fun.
But it's all so extreme no steady degrees
with soaring pollution at all the cars
no public transport and soon the
stars will be covered by planes
making stains of flight lanes
and stopping our breathing again.
Are we ready, is this safe
or clearly for profit and gain?

This unlock time it covers her dreams
The peace for a short time she knew.
So just for today she's feeling blue
Don't worry she'll find something to do
To deny her human cry -
Keep herself going like you.

A Midsummer Prayer

Oh, Lord above and Lord below -
In this Midsummer Solstice glow -
Bring light to our minds,
Bring warmth to our hearts,
the Gods of many voices.
Oh, Father Sky and Mother of the Seas
and the God of your choice whoever it be,
Make us wiser make us freer, steadily
Unlock us now for us to see how
locked down we've been in our humanity.
Bring the light of this longest night of the year
To unlock and unpick silently
Unravel our opinions,
our flags staking claims,
with our own empire gains -
Let us start again,
surrender step fully
risking humility.
Enlighten, light up, our humanity
And help us in our responsibility
to hold this earth respectfully.

A Three Sticks of Make-up Rule

The wrinkles are coming in -
Coming in two by two
Making patterns on the skin
and I can't do anything.
Some say it's all about wisdom
I don't need to know I'm wise
I'd simply prefer to disguise myself
in a place where old age is despised.
Those lines march along steadily
and the crows fly around my eyes
my face clearly shows that time's
played its games, years have stolen by.
But I never will compromise
over any facade that lies
over any cosmetic cover up
that hurts the planet and eats the pockets
of those who try to take time back
and plaster over the cracks.
So here I stand ageing and tall
and for my next zoom call
have a three sticks of make-up rule
saying: Let those lines show all.

Miners of Gold

Each day brings a new identity,
something somehow you couldn't see -
when life was just too busy.

It may be a thought that preoccupies you
a fear you might not handle it all
this surreal time in an upside-down world
when really you know it's always been there
covering something deeper inside
a kind of gut fear.

But what if you let it accompany you
and in the layers exposed
you one day find a capacity
for something creative, bold
an opening where there seemed to be nothing
shining at you in the dust-coated folds
of an old miner's jacket cast-off and sold.

It isn't iron and it isn't rust
it's a source of gold and the rock needs tapping
something extracting with pick and hammer

from fossilised layer
layer upon layer of self-imposed labels
and of course you still fear
what's found deep down lying there
beneath the foothills under the ground in that
untamed land.
And that's the surrender
those miners of gold
had on Route 49.

Barefooted

On the edge of the sand,
where it meets the sea,
in this empty land,
there's you and me
standing silently
barefooted,
watching the waves gently
easing our insecurities.
Feeling the water
rising and falling
over rounded contours
the bony ridges and fleshy valleys
of our sand soft feet
and laughing
laughing to feel our infancy
a bellyful laugh deep chuckling within
at the teasing of the tide
tickling our skin
on the edge of the sand
where it meets the sea -
in this empty land, there's you and me.

A Kind of Identity Rap

He tried so hard to please his mum,
right from the very start -
but it came at a price:
he gave up on himself
and offered his mother his heart.
The die was cast.

We need the connecting the loving the bonding
before we have speaking, before we have thinking
and our mother loves us, holds us tight
but for many of us it just doesn't feel right.
She's easily distracted, not truly connected
too much to do to be with you
this little baby who needs her so
who will give his all not to let her go
an instinct, primal in infant bones.

So he clings to his mother who's on her phone
and his mum is scared at this intimate touch
she's never felt love so she panics confused.
It's all too much:
she covers it up all in this functional stuff.

Feed, wind, change his nappy
put down to sleep, I wish he'd sleep
"Quality Time" try to get it right
exhausted from waking up in the night.

And that small bundle soaks it up
his mother's feelings whatever they are
blames himself and makes her his star.
It's not a decision he's too young to decide
he's just a baby - it's unconscious inside.
He becomes his mother in order to survive
hears his mother's sad laughter
and becomes a 'good' child
no sign of anger, no sign of tears
dissociated through the years
to keep her safe the one he needs
his mum in her bubble disconnected
full of trauma he'll carry for her.

So he plays and keeps that role
all through his life as he meets others
gives up on himself and cares
for them well. It makes him feel good
and comforts his empty soul.

Until he discovers something's not right

It's usually a lover and they're starting to fight
she triggers his trauma, flirts with his fear
controls where it hurts and makes him hers.
So he goes to therapy starts to see deeply
his disguises, how he's survived -
who he has had to be.
And in his query what's far more scary
is who he is and wants to be.

He sheds the clothes chosen by another
slowly discovers, uncovers the layers
of all these things he's learnt.
And the more he starts to be secure
loves who he is and speaks his truth
he just breathes and feels healthy and well.
No image, no mask, no need to impress.

We need leaders like this.

Laugharne, Wales
August 2020

What did Dylan Thomas see
when he cleaned his boots and polished his tea
and looked out at this estuary?

Wrapped in this timeless history, I watch
curlews stiffened on sticks of stilts
strut and stagger across the strand ungainly
on messy black mudflats daily
that make shifting moments of land appear
in the rising and fall of tides through the year,
recall mud pie hands sticky and grey with
hours of my childhood play.

And four of them come this morning
Four of them in the low flow mud water
strutting slow with a croo-we-cree
heard in the sounds of the estuary
peering and spearing quick with a flick with
long beaks curved carefully
catching the prey of this late August day
watching wearily.

One runs fast towards another clumsily really
like the stilts are a liability
and the beak just doesn't belong to her
not the well-measured pace of a heron's grace
bead-like eyes on the fish he spies pierced by the
    kill.

She runs, this curlew, too quickly
falling over herself just slightly ungainly
and the others fly away suddenly
three gone now passed
she's left alone to fish for more
to strut the shore
in that minute or two between
our toast and coffee.

Is this what Dylan Thomas could see
as he cleaned his boots and polished his tea?

Laugharne 2
August 2020

Lush the grass today
Strips of apple green shade
blades in the breeze
and streaks of bright lime
as the sun lights the sky
paints the palette of early morning
fresh and glistening.
And the leaves dapple flecked
in the damp hazel trees spit dry
flickering free in a calmer wind
the night's gale gone passed on.

I wake at seven forget where I am
rubbing my eyes in a half-dream
as the sunlight pours in
softening the walls
with a new hope and peace
an emptying
all troubles gone made free again
by this great flow of water, flowing forever estuary.

The tide's going out, meandering
with a rush in the centre that twelve hour thing
and wisps of the Gower
far out there
that changes with the weather
like the clouds in the air
scudding the sky playing with the sea
bringing pattern to the land
a tapestry of texture mixture of colour
nature's blended so skilfully.

And the mudflats striated in changing light
curving and sweeping from left to right
carved to the ebbing
with water flowing and ancient knowing -
a woven wonder to an artist's eye
mud fleshy, flesh fickle to the changing tides.

The water ripples in steady pace
wrinkles of an old man's mortal face
and the sparkle of his eyes when he sees it all
sees how it glitters bedecked with jewels
as the wind and tide controls the pull.

Oystercatchers flock
on the mud banks waiting

like village women anticipating,
smelling the weather coming downwind
chatting together birds of a feather
And the heron hides in the clump of reeds
Can you see it's there still
by the rusty iron crow's nest
rests from hours of diving and fishing,
still there, statue still.

This beautiful sweeping estuary
Whisper of Wales made bold by words
doesn't need poetry, not really, not me
when the poet of this nation did it so well.
The estuary says nothing holds silent wondering
at the thousands of years that have gone beyond
with no building in site it's just the same
none of it changed.

It quiets the mind makes us breathe tame
stills the soul, calms our agony
a time out of life to reflect deeply
on the year's insanity.

And the field mouse darts in
goes out with the cheese
A flicker in life's history.

Berlin Ten Days Ago
September 24, 2020

I see the smile of shiny red
lips glistening with gloss
a child's sweet paper crinkled
and dropped on the path
past the bridge
on Kottbusser Damn
and green broken glass
it makes me smile too
in this early morning September sun
mask-less and happy
task-less and free
lucky to see my son again
after so long in captivity.

Walking by the banks of the canal
swans of eight float in lined formation
how do they know to keep
distance between them
the one point five metre rule
such accuracy
dignified, graceful and slow.

If they wore masks too,
I get the feeling
they'd still know how
to go with the flow.

Unlocking Waterstones

So books now need time to self-heal
They'll be put on a tray piled up all neat
And wheeled away
isolated on retreat
Taken from the seat of learning
for three days of rest
from the daily digesting
of readers
who decide not to buy
inspect and reject
then agree to deny them a loving home
or a place to roam from one hand to another
friends passing on
which brings smiles to their cover
when their readers gasp, gasp to discover
the mystery, the thriller, the name of the killer
the intrigues of lovers
explorers' adventures
books about trees, books about sleaze
exposed social horrors in pithy plots
and such a lot more in the turning of pages

that earn these books their wages.
So now it's hard times if you're on the shelf
You're card and paper after all
and the stories you hold as you're pulled down and mauled
get forgotten in these covid days
Like some fun has gone in your secret play as
you now see the fear in your readers' eyes
distracted from plot by hands sanitised.
You suffer you books that are hot off the press
I can feel your distress
as they pick up another
and seal your fate cast aside to wait
And you're put on a heap
in alphabetical order
in a book's lockdown stock.
Sent off on a 72 hour detox
Quarantined, unseen for hygiene's sake
to get clean, rehabilitate.

The Old Apple Tree
*In memory of the Abercairn Apple Tree,
cut down for housing development*

Apples fallen felled by the wind
bruised and wet from the rising dew
shine in the sunlight new and skin rosy
with October mist full wispy and hazy
still warmth in the breeze not yet cold.
Apple trees heavy bearing a load
bent-backed branches till the apples
picked are gathered in baskets
for peeling and coring
pressing and juicing
pickled or for freezing
seizing this time of harvest fruit feasting.
Some rotten with worms tunnelling and boring
some ready for bobbing at Hallowe'en
if that's still okay with clean hygiene.

This English love of the apple tree
the blossom and bud,
the fruit ripe and ready,
this love keeps us steady
nature's history

in our rolling hills and satanic mills
the root of abuse predicted by Blake.
Our apple trees make our identity
fruit sent from Kent
and in the south west
pressed into cider in Somerset.
Cider with Rosie and Laurie Lee
Our revolution of industry
Factory upon factory, car upon car -
carbon emission bringing apples from afar,
New Zealand and Chile,
Yet in our backyard
we've forgotten our tradition
the lungs of our garden
the old apple tree.
It's dying, it's dying in front of our eyes
House upon house will cause its demise
Apple that gave us the knowledge of life
innocence gone to bring toil and strife
all that's conceived in Adam and Eve
lovers together, lovers apart
the knowledge held close to impart.

Whatever else, what warms my heart
is the sight of the Russet, the Lady of Bath
The Gala, the Courtland, the Ginger gold

and a cox or two for me to hold
Three hundred years they're species of old.
And the baked Apple pies you had as a child
covered with custard, warming inside
all this is still there in our countryside.
It's something we seem to have deemed to deny
as we open the plastic-wrapped food we buy.

All of us, them and you and me,
We just have to look we just have to see
Look with our eyes at the nature still
Look at the waste where apples fall
Look how kids reject fruit with a bruise
unblemished according to mass market rules.
We've lost our connection with soil and with land
And it's changing changing we see what we've done
So let's eat as the seasons the food as it comes
Let's pick from the hedgerow, forage the paths
keep our allotments and be subversive
slow down and do things differently.
Let's not lose our identity
so many varieties gone forever
Let's fight for the old orchard apple tree.

Section 3:

TIERS OF TEARS

Just bellow...!

There is no place you can go, actually
There is no place like the wild roaring sea
to echo your shouts
and screams so.
It listens attentively somehow,
somehow it seems to know.
Call back,
you cry and you bellow
with anger and joy
as it lashes and turns you
excites and thrills you so.
Just let go
strip yourself free in the cold morning air
and the sea will hear
hear your bold roar
as you run through the rollers
toes curled with cold.
There is no place you can go
but the sea will hear you bellow.
It roars with you in the dawning light
stays till the end of your waking day
and in your sleep you hear it still

it's infinite might and will
to be with the pull
moon to tide, tied to moon
it heals your aching soul.

Humour me

It's really disgusting,
shocking, but not
that there are people lusting
to make a quick buck
from this Covid-19 -
give jobs to the boys
so they play with their toys
within the circle of the powers that be
the public servants at the top
of this our political hierarchy.
Let that go down in history.

It may have been urgent,
but that's not good enough –
where is the transparency
where is there any decency
when a businessman from overseas
makes twenty-one billion pounds
as a go-between agent buying PPE
for our NHS staff on such low pay,
securing a contract none of us see?
Twenty-one billion raised from our taxes

the taxes of many that now have no job
in debt in a lockdown misery.

It's clear they'll be vast profits made
in the pharmaceutical industry
And it's just a naive fantasy
to ask that all the profits made from the vaccines
and all the companies that supply PPE
made into heroes by Public Relations -
more dubious connections and contracts of corruption –
to ask that all the profits made from this pandemic
taken from our taxes
goes to those now living in poverty.

Just humour me a little, humour me
It's just my naive fantasy.

Perished at sea

Take me to the river
where we can hourly see
a bridge passing over
that murky brown water
where the homeless take cover
from the rain and cold
and the current forever
ageless and old
flows timeless and free.

Take me to the river
which journeys to the sea
tides with shreds of silver
And planes flying over
to land so easily.

Here someone's story
is bartered and sold
here they feel numb water
see sky turn dark and gold
here they gather together
storm brewing in the weather

in a boat overloaded
all crammed in together.

Take me to the water
where there's fear in their hearts
Their babies are crying
to make a new start
in a country with possibility
where they'll stop your journey
if they can. The authorities.

Take me to the water
where you who love each other
needlessly perish at sea
your bodies swept up on
a beach somewhere
for all those lucky to stop and stare
another statistic for us to hear
an echo of hope
coming from the water
surrender your lives for security.

Take me to the water
where a person may swim
Some may surf and there's kayaking
A dog jumps the waves

and fishermen sing.

Take me to the water for me to think
how countries meet together
mapped link by link
how the sea flows forever
and a boat out there may sink.

A Sleep Memory –
Khartoum 1978

Rainy season again.
The Nile filters have clogged up
and there's no water in the tap.
All soaped down but no shower today
Rain lashing down and we're sweaty hot.

So we throw our towels off and run outside
we scream in our fortunate privacy,
the shower from the skies the best they'll be.

It beats our skin with its pummelling
making us laugh making us feel
the relief and cooled down ecstasy.

The rains have come streets pitted and full,
with muddy lakes and old planks for boardwalks
and still the goats scavenge and wild dogs stalk.

Eritrean refugees camp under skins outside our
 house
on the large void land you could call a road.

They have no fortunate privacy,
just tin pans to cook on open fires in the potted
    holes
but not for now
the rains beat down
and throughout this great town
where Blue Nile meets White Nile
the filters are clogged up.
There's no water in the taps.

Lockdown recipe

Take a handful of lockdown days
Put them in any bowl strong and sturdy
Stir in a dollop of government advice … slowly
Add two eggs from one household only
A pinch of cumin and turmeric
and a whole hot chilli to spice it up.
Dance to music as you cook
just shake your arse and move those hips
with the recipe book propped up to see
dog-eared all messy at page twenty-three.
Add 200 grams of TV news and pound it a bit.
Best of course with a pestle and mortar
until it's completely gone to powder.
Throw in an hour of exercise daily
to the point where it feels hot and sweaty
breathing rapidly.
Mix it all together with a sprinkle of statistics
to make it elastic and thick in texture
Then form small balls in your hands
using up all the lockdown mixture
do it slow and carefully
they could fall apart easily.

Fry until brown and you smell the aroma
opening the windows if you cough a bit
And remember to check your temperature.
before making the sauce to accompany it.
Watch out for bubbles, keep stirring of course
that goes without saying with sauce.
Cover the lockdown balls while they're hot
pouring the sauce to cover the lot
then plate them up. Serve immediately.

The Dance of Intimacy

Some people live two metres apart anyway
Nothing to do with these lockdown days
Others live close to another's heart
and that's where they stay.

Then there are those who come too close
persuasive and invasive
impose and suppose in a subtle way that they know.
They always look kind when they want to rule
keep control, make others small
and we trust them then realise actually
they're not to be trusted at all.

And there are some who can't do any of this
want their desert island bliss
the radio choices are their dream
and the further away from others they go
well, that feels safer, less stressed.

And some will mould themselves like clay
cover and fold themselves away in another's skin
never come out of hiding.

Two metres apart is too far away
life's risk and dare makes them full of fear
whatever the cost they prefer to be lost
in another's life. Separation is hell.

Measured precision is the lockdown rule
to keep us healthy and well
But it sets me thinking about relating
what it feels to be distanced or too near
and somehow there's a balance in it all
between close and apart
a breathing in and breathing out
a dance in the infinite figure of eight
which feeds the human heart.

Forbidden Fruit
Christmas Memories

I always looked for that flat one back then,
with a delicate twisted twirl at each end -
the fanciful dancer of pantomime -
bright yellow shining with tree light lustre
star among the colours all loud and garish
with a magic wand for my taste buds.
That half-eaten purple-blue tin
a one-way direction up Quality Street
a Christmas treat with no U-turn –
those tins were much larger and deeper then.

Children's hands delving, eyes looking in
goading each other grabbing and seizing
claiming the one unique to us
the shape of our favourite, a silent sweet
secret, our secret, not wanting to tell
for fear a brother caught on and
held tight teasingly.

Someone's got it already I can see
there's the crunched-up paper over in the bin
Oh, I'm hoping, hoping, hoping, hoping

there's one remaining under them all.
Got it. Grab it. Take it quick.
Don't stop and look in again.
Can't hang around in a large family -
it's me and you but right now it's me.

I don't like the feeling on my skin unwrapping
that rustling cellophane but I'm cursing my fingers
clumsy with hurry and haste for the stake
claimed, taken, and oh for the taste
my tongue curls round the toffee smooth and tough
it takes patience to suck all those pleasures in
caressing my lips lush the juices within.

And I feel that first time of relishing when later
I open that metal tin and steal a sweet again.
It starts a wish for forbidden knowledge, a fantasy
secreting the taste of the toffee remaining
and my sticky lips my sticky skin
sign of a feast on seductive pleasure the taste of
   secret sin.

You couldn't get sin from a plastic container with
parents hovering
back then they were too busy to notice anything
and it had to be a deep metal tin.

Anger

Wild old man
Watery eyed
Why so angry
Trebling up three tiers or more
on each wave you bring
rolling them in with such fierce attitude?
What's eating you, are you feeling it too
unruly sea, the anger
we can't right now express?
You crash and you lash as you meet my feet
Your white roaring mane
too powerful
Venting your foamy spleen
Sensing the chaos the world is in
I'll step back - let your raging in.
Let the madness show in your silver white wave
and soapy suds of my father's chin
Watery eyed
Wild old man -
Wise I mean.

Section 4:

NO ENDGAME IN SIGHT

Shifting in -tion

Increasing frustration
Sad with recollection
Loss of friend connection
Digital obsession
Angry reaction
Unhealthy seduction
Scientific refutation
Crazy distraction
Fearful palpitation
Meaningful communication
Communal intention
Creative recitation
Focused meditation
Positive affirmation
Fun recreation
Laughter and relaxation
Music and television
Grateful dedication
Nothing more to mention
That's me.

Cocktail Bitter and Sweet

This lockdown thing
feels like nothing - and everything
Like seeing my life through a magnifying glass
distorted and convex
until I get close, look in.
Where all that I've done all that I've been
are here undone, gone
memories shown on a movie screen
in this in between time
from one life to another we're in.
I'm sad and smiling
cocktail bitter and sweet
at how life is flying
a fleet of recollections.
And they say you get this when you're dying
your life on a reel in your mind's eye
all that you've been
the making of heaven and hell within.
Love that's been real and Plato's delusions
Just everything there before your eyes
the hurt, the joy, the compromise.
All you can hope is that someone's beside you
to hold your hand as you say goodbye.

Porridge
January 2021

As I stir the porridge in the pan,
A multitude of eyes pop up -
Eyes of gargoyles on gothic churches,
The gurgling of lava in deep volcanoes
And the play of marbles on pavements grey
As they click, collide and roll away.

I'm mesmerised by the bubbling patterns,
forming a skin and
scalding the side of the pan
with brown crusty line.
Hypnotised by the glittering winter mornings
the smell of coke in stoked-up stoves -
Jack Frost patterns I see again with a
child's eyes on the window pane
making me cosy and safe inside.

The Portal

When this is all over,
I just wonder - will I want to make
that very first step out the door once more?
Will I have the trust that it's over and dusted
when the powers that be say okay?
Do they really know anything anyway?

Although we yearn to hug and kiss
hold our friends again, be together
in the trauma of what we've been through
we may be core-frozen, stay away -
keep to the distance ingrained in us
and still get stuck in the Covid way.
Or maybe we've enjoyed this space
Have fear that we'll rush back to old ways,
Actually want the simple life
Unwilling to face the madness again.

Doors are a portal from old life to new:
On the day when we make our first step out
Of course it won't be so black and white,
but will some stay in and some walk through?

Silent soft space

Palm to rock, rock to palm
May I find you in the space between
In the silence and space where no face can be seen
the warmth in between
where all life can be.
The rock will guide me to lay my hands there
Smooth it cupped bare
Cup it smooth
Caress the roughness
Of ancient rock skin
The imperfections of weathering
Palm to rock, rock to palm
May I find you in the space between
In the silent soft space where no face can be seen
I lost you just now
but I know you're here
my mind unloose with wandering
how can I hold my hands in prayer
if I don't feel the warmth in between
the heat of aching longing.
Palm to rock, rock to palm
I'll stay with you here

if just for a while –
simply being.

Stained Glass Man

Locked in a circle of glass, he's searching,
searching for a way of escaping -

He writes a song in the key of G
but the sounds aren't right –
dissonant tones that are more like a minor
words that take flight.

He sighs to himself
hears the plight in his voice
the crack of fear that's embedded in there
like a shard of glass sharp
with lack of choice.
This lockdown is real

He's stuck in here
stretching his arms, stretching his legs
to reach the black lead
imprisoning him
right now like barbed wire
incarcerating these lanky

limbs suffocating, holding him in.

His role to be this suffering beauty
set somewhere in a piece of
stained glass, rising up
sacrifice to a piece of art
stuck like a fly in Polish amber
with crystals that slumber
and the light shining through in coloured hues
changing the colour of his skin
A fragile glass man locked in.

Cot Poems

1
He kept her locked in a parakeet's cage -
All night she screeched and squealed,
Covered her eyes and couldn't see -
A baby shouldn't know such things;
A baby shouldn't know.
She froze as she felt her keeper's hands
Froze in her tender young soul
He had the key to her freedom
but by day she flew beyond
to a land of infant magic
where a spark of light could be found.
No-one protected her from the dark.

2
Her father echoed her sobbing sound.
It was dropped in the curve of a wave
Thrust and thrown and churned around
Stranded in a far off bay.
She searched in every weary shell
scattered near and far
The echo she has never found
lost in the tidal draw

One day for another to understand
but never be known by her.

3
She knows it now this secret kept -
It liberates her soul -
And she can find her voice again,
no muffled sound or tightened throat
no retching, spewing, giving in
her breath no longer held.
Her eyes no longer screwed up tight
It's here,
here she affirms the baby within
who lived a fraternal hell.

Water

1
Am I Water, as the card says
Actually am I
fluid and free soft and powerful?
I know 60 per cent of me is you
H2O. You, the solvent of life
You, with your hundred ways to
keep me alive,
deliver, convert, flush and lubricate
protect all that's inside
dissolve, warm and cool me.

2
To you we should bow –
Make your rivers and streams
a Deity, revere them somehow.
I went to the June festival
close by the Schuylkill River
in South Street Philadelphia
where fruit and flowers are thrown in
made as an offering
to the Yoruba goddess Oshun

bringing a good New Year in.
They bow at Varanasi
India's holiest city
to the great flowing Ganges
a God to those who bathe in her
purified by her murky waters.
There the divine can be found.
I bathed bound by clothes
where she reaches the sea
where the tiger dwells
in the Bay of Bengal.
Cupped my hands like a font for baptism
splashed water all over
cleansing myself to start again.

3
Precipitation again and again,
sustainer of all life on, in and above.
The cycle of rain we all moan about
We should love and respect you
Have the right to taste you clean
Not polluted by dirty industry
Not eco irresponsibility
Not dirty and dangerous from poverty
But clean as a spring
'Water gin clear' as they say in the Fens.

4
The sprites of the water have tales to tell
of life below in the reservoirs and hidden lochs,
where eels six foot long bury themselves
and monsters dwell and bellow.
Where church bells are buried
heard ringing at night
Villages hidden long lost valleys
the school, and the hall and memorial.

5
The sea whispers sweet notes to me
sometimes roars impatiently
In naked harsh winds it tells me
to listen, come close and see
I offer myself to this wet wild pathway
that touches each country bound by a sea
to waves rough clapping, laughing and lapping
Smell the salty quality different daily
freezing ice cold or temperate warm.

6
I read the word Water on the card again
See TEA in the letters, that mug of hot drink
I always want when I come in
Hands frozen embrace and trace patterns

with stiff little fingers feeling
the tingling tips of my skin.
And then I read RAW in water
feel the sting the moment you hurl yourself in.
The burning.

7
I've lined the dried out plants in a row
Ready for watering.

Kimonos, Bears and Milonga

You can see how simple my life has become
when I ask myself this as I walk home –
have you ever thought of cheating
on the steps on your phone when you see
the reading says five thousand, feels more like ten
and right now you feel all in.
There's no competition except with myself
but still I consider stealth.
Think I may find a kimono
dress myself tight as a geisha girl
make delicate steps like the flutter of wings
as a butterfly passes by.
Or maybe if that's a bit far-fetched
take myself back to those poems for the young
and remember those lines I can't step on
where the bears come out on a London street
and eat you up, you succulent meat
cause your steps are too long
and you don't stay in those squares.
And if none of that works to
make my steps shorter

I'll take myself back to the tango hall
in close embrace partner to partner
short steps as I move quick-paced
as I dance the beach boardwalk backwards
in heels tango black like Ginger Roger's
and we do the milonga my beat getting stronger
to the strains of sultry Piazzolla.
You'd double your data in half the time
cover those days you stay inside
Train yourself for that cheating heart
Smile and laugh as people look on
and you do a street shuffle, skuttle along.

Then you stop, think no harm in all of this
and a hell of a lot of innocent fun
but hold on a moment – actually
who am I cheating on?

Unmasked

You do not have to be perfect, you know,
keep yourself tight and correct
hold your shoulders high and padded
wadded with steel and mesh.
You just have to feel the rumble in your belly
the jelly-like fear,
the tenderness,
the fold of the arms that try to embrace you,
the soul of another,
who thaws your control -
the one who is there and slowly unmasks you
and warms your confused caress.
You do not have to be perfect, you know,
to feel how another's love
can infect
your ancient loneliness.

The magic of a can of spray

This is a poem for the Piston Broke
I'm not a bloke like all of you
but there's a can I'm partial to
that's yellow and blue
with a tinge of red and white.
Bet you've guessed it already
the sheer quality
Yes, the WD40
For me it was love at first sight.

This gem of a spray is a must
It removes oil, dirt and dust
Cleans and protects from rust
Prizes apart male and female threads
Screws that get stuck together too tight
This humble can kept out of sight
always sets everything right.

Water **D**isplacement had **40** tries
They tried so hard and produced a prize.
which somehow makes me warm inside
and happy when things get really stuck

to have a spray that opens things up
greases and lubricates all that stuff
That rain and rust mess up.

Fixed to the cap
they have a new straw
They call it the Smart straw like a phone
just why I'm not sure
but this straw is clever
because as you squirt
it helps you direct the jet with precision
stops it making a stain dripping down the wall
or soiling your skirt as you stand in the rain
with no rag at hand and start to complain
at the bolt that's stiff on the garden gate
that needs your mate called WD
this can of spray that makes you free.
Well, you don't need no man
to go running to
can do it yourself
not thwarted but sorted.

So thanks to the workers of San Diego CA
my beret comes off to them any day.
For the way they produce
something warm in me

when I see that can with the bright red cap
which gets me out of many a fix
with all its lubricant tricks.

Somehow it always saves my day
The man in the can of magic spray.

Salvage

It's like summer today
and the blue sky unbroken
from here to the horizon
brings joy to this garden by the sea.
Nature has spoken, no lock-up for her
she's busy spring-coming and up for rebellion
moving about and on the run, fresh and flirty.

Birds working and singing and life in the air
bulbs showing green heads in the warming earth
birth in the fields and it can't be stopped.
Not like us.

We could fall off the planet and would she care
Would she miss all our damage and human fuss
Or just salvage what she needs from
the remains of us
and pick herself up.

Winter swim

Cruel beast, you got me
you pompous pretender,
cutting me with your bitter freezing
razor sharp easterly. A Siberian swim.
Beast from the East, vicious hound
howling across the strand
untethered, unruly, on the run
you whipped round my body and even after
the sea and the ice and the waves were done
there was nowhere to hide
from your menacing. No covering.
Biting at my front. Biting at my back.
Even the wrapping of towelling
dry robed and warm in normal times
held no shelter.
The tips of my bloodless fingers stung.
I dried as flakes of snow started falling
every last part of me numb
and speechless with each laboured breath
breathless puffs of mist, smoky vapour.
Without voice I found
no words for the crystal pebbles,

no words for the frost shrivelled seaweed
no words for the gulls that are turned to stone.
It was sheer survival that kept me dumb.

The moon is mourning

It was late at night
The moon without lights
Looked like half a heart suspended in the sky
Sad without life
And the fear inside
was has nature around me already died?
And the moon is forewarning
its need for mourning
Looking at us in the streets below
No sweet moon face now
no trace of picture book
But angry with chiding
that we've known so long and done nothing
that in our deriding of all that is green
we haven't heard haven't seen
the bird song gone the insects blown away
poisoned on all that spray.
Is there still hope for another day?

Cod Liver Oil and Frogspawn

The frogs have laid frogspawn in the pond
marking the start of spring
I saw them mating endlessly
So it's no surprise to me.

It's like a grey cover of bubble wrap
All shiny as jelly with lots of cells packed
plastic wrapped bubble protecting black dots
thousands of alien eyes looking up.

Then those eyes grow tails
Sperm stuck inside capsules
Cod liver oil we had as kids
Yuck do you remember all lined up
to keep us from colds disgusting stuff.

A cover of ice forms late in the season
spawning tears frozen and you wonder now
will they recover, somehow survive
this bitter weather.

Then the tears start to flow
and you know the thaw's coming
will bring them back.
Nothing but eggs that's all you can see
Cod liver oil and frogspawn
writhing to be released.

Nature's time capsules wriggling in weeds
Bursting with will, new life swimming free.

OTHER POEMS

Lockdown Fantasy

Hanky Panky
Lockdown time
I went through his window
he went through mine
and I have to say what happened there
was worth the £30 fine

Guitar Pick

I spot the white pick and feel happy
It has brought itself here to Germany
Sits on the carpet in my Air B&B
Staring up at me.
I didn't pack my plectrum not got my guitar so I've
no idea how it's got right there
and the teasing pleasure it gives to me is a memo of
home and how I like to be
with time just for me playing my guitar.
Somehow my pick's jumped into my case
and stakes it's place in my heart.
At first I blink and kind of think I've imagined it
then I pick it up check to see
just a small white plectrum
a plastic tear, moment of home
makes me happy
sitting alone
in a house I don't know
in a Strasse in Berlin.

"Roses are red, my love"

Violets are blue
Sugar is sweet, my love
But not as sweet as you.

So why don't you put your socks in the bin
Why leave the lid off the biscuit tin
Always forget to lock the front door
Leave the shower mat on the bathroom floor
And when I've been out having some fun
The washing up is still left undone.
Why do you leave on the kitchen light
when we've gone to bed
wasting energy all through the night.

But hey, enough said, talking of bed
My rant is over and you're a pain
But I love you all the same
I'm off to bed I hope with you
Let's have a cuddle or two.
Cause roses are red my love
Violets are blue
Sugar is sweet my love

But not as sweet as you
Remembering you live here too.

My Pesce Way

I call myself a pescatarian with a
pork pie eating habit.
Don't know what it is but, when I'm in the Co-op,
I walk down the aisle where I know it's there
and do a kind of u-turn like the basket turn in jive,
then I have to grab it like a fox with a rabbit
Just can't let it go.
Against all my convictions and environmental
    reasons
that pork pie jumps from my hand to the basket
and I feel some satisfaction
a kind of salivating, a licking of the lips
at the catch I've made as I hunted it down.

It's not like it's a grand one -
No pork pie from a classy deli
no food snobbery for me – not really -
but it's hidden at the bottom of my black plastic
    basket
under the beetroot and the leafy green kale.
I never asked it in there, must belong to another
but it doesn't you see. It belongs to me

and there is no swapping the secret of my shopping

So if you meet me in the Ham Road Co-op,
and I don't want to stop, look down kind of
shameful a veggie like me
as I cover something up -
You'll know it's my day,
for wandering astray down the row in that store
opposite the hummus where the pork pies allure
my palate and play.

What a strange life, sad you could say,
When it makes my day to break my pesce way.

Gallahers

A tin the colour of boot polish.
Buff writing and round in my mind.
I search for the name in the fog of my brain.
That's it. Gallahers. Rich Dark Honeydew.
Tom Gallaher Irish Tobacco King
and my father's favourite brand.
He'd twist it open, it crackled in his fingers
a few clumps rich brown with a spring in the
    strands,
he'd pack his pipe and tamp it down.

The crinkled dry leaves of tobacco plantations
imported and stripped out by women's hands
'strippers' of a different kind who
went to dances all washed down,
but the men knew where they worked in town.

His pipes were stacked on the pipe rack
a nest of joy in the bowl at the end
of the tarred stems. The Bryant and May matches
hiss as they flash. Alight. The test draw
draw in, puff, draw in, puff and the engine ignites.

Smoke fills the car as we sit at the back all
packed together – no seatbelts of course- and Dad's
cough hoarse.

Smoke at the windows and on our chests
familiar traces the comfort of being
his secondary smoker. No one knew then
it was just pipes and men
and Bohemian women looking like Indians.
My mother sometimes complained
but my Grandad, my Dad and my Brother
Pipes and baccy were done back then.

The smog became fog and he couldn't
see so he wound down the window in the car
as we were going I don't know where
and we were hit by the frozen air
our lungs in shock.

Pipes and packing and playing with pipe cleaners
we could shape into anything.
The tapping on leather his
upturned shoe all polished new and sparkling.
An everyday ritual watched by us
no nicotine fingers or cigarette papers
just my father's way to light up and relax.

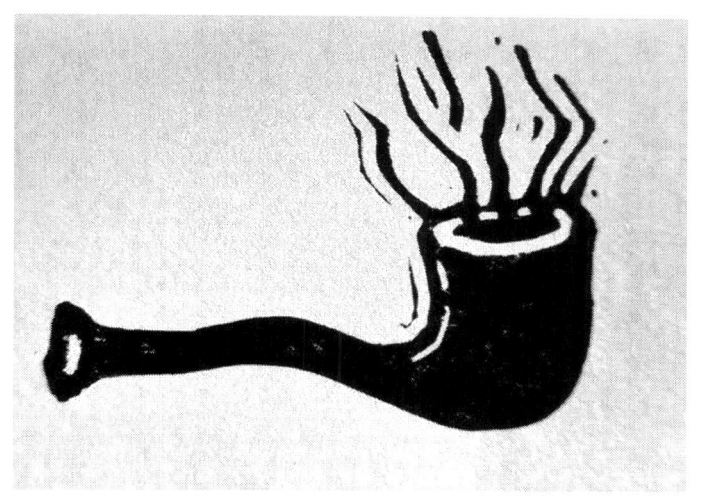

A Shepherd Woman in Wales

This woman appeared out of a hedgerow as I was walking down a Welsh country lane in 1973 and I've never forgotten our conversation.

Have you ever met an old battered woman
In the winds of autumn,
Stooped with her oil potato sack
Draped round her sagging skin, sallow and sour,
Willing her way along a country lane -
Searching for unknown faces, familiar, forgotten.

She cries out in pain,
Bent at the knees
As her doubled frame reaches for nettles
To take home for tea.

Stones

When my sister was down
and my sons were young
she'd walk the beach searching
for holy stones and they'd follow along.
Pebbles with holes in the middle
weighing our pockets down.
We'd tie them on string hanging in order.

In the wind, I heard the stones sing.

Stone stupas stood on Iona
The island of Columba.
Stood stone upon stone
mindfully balanced by walkers passing.
With reverence we walked round them
clockwise. They were saints standing steady
the unsung heroes common people
in housing estates their stories untold

In the wind I heard them speak bold.

In medieval times stones hung round the neck

of condemned men or witches thrown in
drowned, innocent or not. And still
today in some countries men who may covet
a man's wife in the silence of fantasy
judge women severely for committing adultery.
Think they have the righteous right
to take the life of a woman who has none

In the wind the stones cried out.

Stones are unique can a twin be found
Identical in shape and size
Markings the same, no compromise.
You could search all your life for
two stones weathered alike.

On hilltop and plain standing stone circles
adorn this country
Great giants of geology
with ancient energy they hold us.
Don't ask why and who put them there.
Just stand in the middle and feel
what they tell you about life's mystery

In the wind you'll hear.

FOMO and JOMO

Sometimes she has FOMO
Sometimes she has JOMO
Alone and happy then lonely.
It's been like that for years now
friends out there and her here.
In 2020, staying at home was easy for her -
missing out was for everyone.
She wasn't the only one to feel free
from searching for space in her diary.
She turns to her friends and they say the same
lifting the restrictions and starting again
is beginning to panic them.
The vaccine brings some security
but also with it anxiety
that as she steps out a bit wobbly
from all those Zoom meetings and family greetings
they'll be flesh to flesh reality.
Has she changed, is she different
can she keep the connection?
Everyone's out there having fun
as they open things up life's on the run
The fear of missing out comes back

Facebook is playing happy families again
and she suddenly feels lonely
she doesn't want to miss out
- or keep up.

Masks, Hips & X-rays

Went for an X-ray the other day
Said: You'll have to speak up
I can't wear
- hearing aids
- glasses
- a cycle helmet
- a mask as well
They'll all fall off and land in the gutter
So it really matters you say
CLEARLY what you want me to do.
I can't see your lips,
don't know how to sign
if I have to roll over,
turn up the volume and give me time.
Don't patronise me make me feel dumb
it's my hip you see as indicated, not my mind.
Just give me thumbs up
to say when I'm done
I can't see, I can't hear but
you know I'm double vaccinated.
I don't want to be old and tolerated -
I'm fed up today.
All these restrictions have gone on too long.

23 inches wide

She's stuck. Out on the street
for a coffee with friends
like you and me and everybody.
A year of shielding passed
she's all spruced up dressed elegantly
excited to see her mates.

She's stuck. All the streets are full
Trapped with no room to navigate
she can't get to her friends at all
as cafes try to accommodate diners al fresco
eating out, the volume of sound all around
overwhelms her. Chatter of orchestra
laughing bassoon, a whining violin and the sound of
a piccolo strangely low.

She's stuck. No-one hears her ask to get through.
Tables and chairs they've invaded the pavements
She needs 23 inches of width that's all
And she matters too much to end up in the gutter
while others don't see her dilemma.

She's stuck. Her friends text to say they'll wait.
Without her, they say, they can't celebrate
she's one of them and has to be there but right now
she's disappeared. Buried by tables and chairs.

She's stuck. Things used to be bad, this is worse.
No space for her and her wheelchair at all
She's stuck on her first date the streets are full
and she wants her fun like you.

Can't you see you'll have to move over a bit?
She's stuck. She can't get through.

*This poem is written for Katie who wants a drink
out with friends like anyone else. Some cities have
removed Blue Badge parking in centres to make
way for outside dining.*

A Song to the Willow

Why win wandering willow
Winding wind-blown willow
Weary with whistling west with worry
Whipped winter wind writhing with woe.
Which way would you go?
Wistful and slow with branches
white whittled from drifting snow
weighed low.
Why wear webbed roots by the water
and hang your branches with weeping so ?

The Real Press

If you enjoyed this book, take a look at the other books we have on our list at
www.therealpress.co.uk

Including the new Armada novel with a difference, *Tearagh't*, by the maverick psychologist Craig Newnes.

Or the modern fairy tales by David Boyle, *Little Outside-in the-Snow and other stories*...

Also our latest **poetry** selection by Simon Zec...

Printed in Great Britain
by Amazon